MW00509439

Dedicated to the last awakened

one to widely benefit humanity.

CONTENTS

Prologue

Humankind has biologically evolved for a long time. Genome research has found that Homo sapiens or modern humans result from gene exchange between Neanderthal and Homo erectus. Unlike animals, humans completed walking upright. The only living things on earth hold up their head to the sky and step on the ground with two feet. Although the lifestyles of modern people slightly hinder the right posture, we have biologically completed evolution.

If so, what do humans live for 21C? Humankind has existed to cultivate and enhance knowledge. Accumulating knowledge cannot be done by animals or gods, only by homo sapiens. Therefore, human beings use language and have short- and long-term memory. Memory and language enable us to communicate and improve our knowledge beyond time and space, which thus develops technology and culture. If so, what should we do next? The answer would be mental evolution. Outwardly we are of the same human form, but each of us has different standards of living, ranging from egoism to altruism. In other words, we are evolving away from animal instinct to mental maturity.

Thus, a developed environment based on knowledge urges us to live an altruistic life. That is the compelling reason why knowledge has been widened and deepened so far. It seems that the time has come for us not to be a slave of the flesh like beasts, but to accomplish spiritual evolution and become real decent humans. This book will describe who we are and why we were born as human beings and the quality and orientation of new humankind that will emerge after COVID-19.

Furthermore, I expect this book could fill the gap which men have been making by collapsing existing common-senses for us to become mentally mature. And this book will present the future of humanity and introduce a methodology to be new humankind. The 'I' mentioned in this book does not refer to the author, but to the subject itself. 'You' also does not mean the reader, but indicates the counterpart of 'I'.

Also, I do not provide further information about the great men mentioned in this book. Their achievements deserve praise. However, I do not expect that readers will be overwhelmed by their authority and jargon or to adhere to the concepts they had established. It is only the knowledge of that day. With that knowledge, we need wisdom now.

Younjeong Kwak

June 2020

South Korea

Chapter 1

A tale for adults

Once upon a time, there was nothing. Suddenly, a concept of 'I' appeared, and it wanted to exist independently. As soon as the existence of a self emerged as a subject, 'I' separated you from me to define myself. It happens like the ambivalence of brightness and darkness.

The elements claiming to be 'I' began to move cha-
otically and fast. They bumped into each other, leaving
scars. Nevertheless, they considered that existing as 'I'
will be better. As its power and speed accelerated, Big
Bang occurred.

And then it all began. Heaven and earth were created, but it took a while for human beings to emerge. Initially, they acted like animals, but the history of humankind has slowly begun to dawn, proving and insisting 'self or ego' with the development of civilization.

Psyche Opening the Golden Box, John William Waterhouse, 1903

At some time, the ego eventually opened Pandora's box. All the evils came out of it. On this planet, 'I' tried to make myself stand out and make the difference more obvious.

To do that, I, my family, my society, or my country have to be better and have more. On the other hand, you, your family, your society, or your country should be worse and have less for sure. So, things like war, poverty, murder, assault, fraud, blame, hatred, despair, etc. inevitably came out.

Once most people were only focusing on their interests, some words began to be heard. In chronological
order, Siddhartha said, "There is nothing to be said as
mine." Then, Confucius said, "What you do not want to
be done to yourself, do not do to others." Socrates also
said, "Know yourself," and Jesus said, "You must love
your neighbor as yourself." Those were called saints
who would be able to speak of self-reflection and con-
sideration of others.

However, individuality has contributed life on earth enriched with art, culture, technology. In 2020, now 'I' can quite freely show off my personality in various ways. Some people have a great deal of money, good looking, renown, or knowledge much more than the others.

However, a question keeps asking us, "Are you happy now?". Humanity has evolved over the years, and now that the ego has been diversely expressed and proven its existence. So, how can we answer that question?

People have developed to the best of their ability, but there seems to be no hope of moving forward anymore. My story will begin right here. If you are interested, please follow me by turning the next page.

Chapter 2

What am I

There have been lots of discussion about the philosophical question of 'what am I.' Aristotle defined, "Man is a social animal." After that, no one has a clear definition yet. It must be challenging to identify a human being by a philosophical proposition. The reason could be given that the human attribute has not been divided into body and soul, or matter and immaterial. It has always been regarded as one.

Therefore, I started thinking about whether humans and animals are the same. Most researchers have studied to link humans to animals' behavior and thinking. In some cases, animal experiments may also precede for new drugs or new cosmetics. The basic premise of these kinds of study is 'humans are animals.' Responses to the human body can be predicted through animal experiments, but human behavior or thought should be considered from different perspectives.

If we can perceive the body related to animals, what about the soul? Any concept can be established through relationships. In this way, we will be able to grasp the idea of the soul by making a relationship between you and 'I' and between humans and god. The 'I' defined by myself and through you put together to stipulate present 'I' horizontally. Also, 'I' can be vertically defined through the relationship of 'I' with gods and ancestors. For this reason, understanding these three relationships should be premised to recognize 'I'.

Human and animal

A simple biological definition of humans would like this as follow. Humans have a mixed diet or omnivorous primates characterized by the erect posture or bipedalism. Primates have large brains compared with the size of the body and an increased reliance on visual acuity and delicate manual dexterity.

This explanation is limited to the human body. But what about the human soul? If humans are higher intelligence using diverse languages, will this represent the soul? If you believe that humans have souls, do we accept that a man consists of both animal body and human soul? To sum up, both material and non-material properties are part of humans. Unfortunately, current science cannot prove the realm of immaterial and so it would not be easy enough to understand that.

Humans are born with a physical body first, and the development of consciousness then happens. Thus, we feel 'this body is me or mine' because we can feel the precise sense of the body as we experience. However, some people have experienced disembodiment or seeing ghosts or even gods. Also, when meditating, some people reach a complete state of consciousness out of the body. Even though it cannot be given scientific evidence, many of us firmly believe in the existence of the soul. Due to the soul, humans have a broad spectrum of desires.

On the other hand, animals obediently follow the order of Nature to adapt to the environment and to preserve the species. As Charles Darwin and Richard Dawkins claimed, a human could be just a vehicle to carry the gene if we only focus on the physical body from a biological standpoint. For this reason, biological research on humans should take here a beat off because the study of the human body has to be distinguished from the soul. From the perspective of the human body, it could be the most natural for us to live in compliance with the rules of mammals. In this regard, I believe that those who have studied living things on earth will give us the correct usage of the body.

Have you heard about reincarnation? If you do not believe it, here are some shreds of evidence as follows: child prodigies, different gifts, un-selectable conditions such as appearance and born environment, and regret and fear right before death. If there is no transmigration, lots of people should complain about what they do not have, now that everything is unfair. The present life begins on the conclusion of the former life. In this way, it might be dim to know that people always want to be better to fulfill their purpose, unlike animals. If nodding here to some extent, you can assume that the human body is like the clothes you are temporarily wearing for this life, and you must take off someday.

It means that you do not have to be angry that someone else has hit the clothing, made it dirty, insulted it, or even other's dress has different color because all of us will change it anyway. The thing is what to do in the present with this garment carrying the soul. In other words, this body is like an avatar to perform what to do on this planet. No matter how much you indulge in pleasure or boast yourself through the body, it cannot be free from aging and dying. Nonetheless, does anyone still want to claim that this body is 'myself'?

To move on to new humanity, we should abandon our prejudices and attachments to the body. Learning the right way of using it will encourage us to prevent problems caused by misleading it and, instead, intensely concentrate on the growth of the soul. The time has come for the soul to evolve and develop because humanity cannot retreat anymore after this pandemic.

You and I

While the human body has evolved for a long time, how did the conceptual 'I' be created? For one concept to be established, a relative one is undoubtedly necessary. For example, the definition of lightness will be convincing, owing to the existence of darkness. The development of languages made concepts to be defined which were vaguely recognized before. After humans had accumulated various experiences in time and space, the idea of 'I' ended up setting itself.

Humanity has cultivated knowledge and culture over the years to insist and prove 'me or myself.' In the meantime, many 'you,' the opponents of 'I,' had to be sacrificed as public, slaves, prisoners, victims. The stronger the conscious 'I,' the higher the sacrifice had to be made. It is as if kings or authority historically sacrificed many people. Most bad incidents come from the actor's self-consciousness. To be more specific, the criminals' motive could be related to the state of 'my' emotional state or 'my' interests.

There are some examples such as: "I needed money," "I want to satisfy sexual desire," "I was frustrated, angry, raging, or stupid," "I did it to be saved," "I did it for my family, my community, or my country." This action leaves miserable agony for both.

On the other hand, the motives for good deeds arise from compassion for others. If 'I' want to help someone, the motivation is probably because the person looks difficult. For instance, when a foreign man seems to be lost and wandering, 'I' can reach out to him for help, spending my time and energy. This action brings joy to both. But only judgment and act for myself are more likely to make 'you' a victim even without recognizing it. And if the action causes danger, society will handle it as a crime.

For this reason, we do not respect those who live only for themselves. Instead, we value those who sacrifice themselves for the benefit of others, unlike animals. The history of humanity for more than 2000 years has shown the countless unfortunate death of great men who desired power, eternal youth, money, and women.

At the same time, there are great men and women sacrificed for many. Thanks to their dedication to change
history and people's minds, our lives could be better
than the past.

Additionally, as knowledge develops, 'I' am prone to
define myself more sophisticated and intelligent. People of the age before medical science came out did not
even know their blood type. But now we can predict in
advance what genetic vulnerabilities we have. Likewise,
the idea of 'I' becomes stronger as the age progresses,
eventually fixing it as an individual logic. In this state,
'I' want to live alone without interference from others.
Likewise, humanity has so far improved a conceptual 'I.'

Then, we have to ask here whether the conceptually almost completed 'I' makes the world a better place
to live. If the answer is negative, it will signify that our
perspective should turn into you, not for me anymore.
It is because there are countless 'you' have been sacrificed to complete me. For example, while 'I' invented a
computer software at university, children in Africa had
to go to the mountains instead of school to pick up cof-

fee beans for a coffee you have drunk every day. How many staff would be working behind the scenes for one Hollywood movie star?

On a narrower scale, nobody can be born without parental devotion. But as growing up, some people easily overlook the fact, starting blaming parents for some reason. That is to say, no life on earth has ever existed without others' sacrifice. Suppose 'I' perceive the sacrifice of 'you' for the existence of 'I' to be established, what should 'I' do next?

Consequently, the world stops here since we still do not see the value and sacrifices of 'you.' In this respect, 'I' need to put myself down and change the perspective of what I can do for you. From now on, 'my' life will be no longer made by myself, but rather, when 'I' live for you, my life will be established by itself.

Human and gods

Life for the ego originates from the law of the jungle. The development of 'I' could trample and break down 'you' as necessary. Rather than leading the wrong way of life, it was just like a process that Humansity had to develop and evolve civilization. But now we understand that life for 'you' is difficult but more noble and sublime than for me alone.

Then let us discuss the gods. Some specific people listen or see the gods—Jesus, God, Allah, Muhammad, you name it. (Siddhartha is not a god but a master of that time.) Sometimes, we read the Bible or listen to the stories of those who talk to gods in person. Their narrative is oriented by 'I' as follows:

"I am the way, the truth, and the life. No one comes to the Father except through Me (John 14: 6)."

"I will inflict My punishment on whom I will, but My mercy encompasses all things (Quran 7:157)."

In this way, the gods said that people would receive salvation or mercy through themselves. However, it implies that he will punish those who do not believe in him or those who hurt his followers. That is the most attractive fact to believers. However, gods distinguish and differentiate you from one who believes in him to another who does not follow him.

God's way of division splits humans. In this regard, people divide others on my side or not. It also results in genocide, collectivism, or terrorism. Based on this ideology, the sacrifices of millions of people in the world have desperately occurred. 'I' the god insists, was so powerful that humans have to stay as weak and helpless 'you'.

As discussed above, self-centered life is close to animals, but altruistic life is probably the most sacred and sublime act that can be practiced as a being. As long as gods firmly insist on the existence of 'I', paradoxically proving they are not entirely mature, a beneficial conclusion to all humanity is hardly expected until the end of the world.

Hence, I believe that time of relying on gods has passed. Humans can come up with practical methods together on how to lead a life in the right way. With these practical actions take place globally, we will be able to anticipate a beneficial conclusion to ourselves for the next generation and even the last human being.

The answer to the question of 'who am I' can fluidly change through the relationship. 'I' is ostensibly a soul covered with an animal body. And its properties change every moment along with thoughts and emotions. The existence of 'I' is not fixed, but we want to believe that 'I' exist. 'I' live the present through a relationship with you. And the past and future are connected through a relationship between gods and souls. So, the ultimate purpose of existence is to be better 'I' now. In the relationship with people and souls, 'I' can mentally grow and create a more mature society. That would be the answer to 'who am I' as a human being.

Chapter 3

Original Sin

If you understand an ego a little more, another query could arise, like why I was born as a human being. The human body can enjoy sensational pleasure, but on the contrary, it cannot be free from disease, aging, and death. So, in human life, joy and pain exist only in different amounts. So, Buddhism used to say that human life is full of suffering. But it is impossible to be free from it without knowing the leading cause. In religion, some efforts have been made to determine the reason. However, no one can so far clarify it because it happened before at the beginning of the universe.

When life is hard and challenging, I have often said that what I did wrong or what my sin was. Abruptly having great physical or mental pains, I used to think that there might be sins that I have not figured out yet. Since we are not free from death and birth, no one will insist that I am perfect and innocent. Also, only would humans love to do good things for others and feel satisfied, unlike the life of the animals. If so, what is the original sin?

In Genesis, God created the heavens and the earth

in the beginning. Then, on the seventh day, he formed a man named Adam, and then a woman called Eve, taking one of his ribs. However, they ate the fruit of the tree of knowledge god prohibited from the serpent's temptation. Therefore, he drove out them (Genesis 1-3). For this reason, human beings have had to pay for the original sin from now on. To sum up, the original sin results from doing what god forbade from the Christian perspective.

In Buddhism, there came a time; the world contracted and then expanded. The beings from the Ābhassara Brahmā world, the third of the nine heavenly realms from below according to Buddhist cosmology, were mostly reborn in this desire sphere world. Since the advent of humankind, they began to commit sins as stinginess, poverty, theft, weapons, killings, lies, etc. had led to people suffering (Dīgha Nikāya 26: 10-17) based on lopsided views. Lopsided view here refers to words and actions based on self-centered thoughts. Nevertheless, the first sin that had occurred in the state of consciousness was due to ignorance. In other words, out of the state of omniscience, ignorance activated a cognition to recognize that consciousness exists, which is the original sin from the Buddhist standpoint.

Moreover, some might believe what you did wrong in youth or the former life owing to being against social norms could have charged with original sin. Likewise, there exist notions of the original sin with a valid reason, and thus, we have tried to do something good for the remission of sins. In this respect, I will here introduce a new theory of the original sin based on 'Chun-Bu-Gyeong: The Holy Scriptures of Heaven'[1].

Long before this universe was created, there were elements as administrators of the Grand Universe in peace. Over time, however, the particles suddenly began to run counter to the way of coexistence. This movement had left a tiny scar on them for numerous eons. After that, depraved energy carried weight and then started to separate from the energy after gathering 30%. Those energies pulled each other with tremendous accelera-

---

1 Chunbukyeong is holy scripture that was orally passed down about 3800 years ago, consisting of 81 characters in Korea. Around 900, scholar Choi Chi-won was translated into Chinese and became known to the world in 1917 by monk Yeon-soo Gye.

tion. That was how the big bang happened.

Thermal energy started to create various matters making up the physical universe, which occupied 30% of the Grand Universe. 4.6 billion years ago, the earth was created, and then, about 4 million years ago, human beings began to appear. Humanity had developed technology and civilization by cultivating and enhancing knowledge until the winter solstice in 2012. By this time, they have formulated theories and reinforced common sense while the universe has produced new matters. It signifies that we become intelligent enough to explain and understand what the original sin was.

And then, we have been facing a period to figure out what we should do with the knowledge and matters since 2013. This planet is like a 1000 times reduced offender institute to teach what we went wrong before existing as souls with the law of the Grand Universe or Nature[2]. That is, to understand what rightness is, every

---

2 Here, the law of Nature refers to the law of heaven, the law of earth, and the law of humans. The law of heaven means the principle of energy that exist beyond tangible materials and the law of the earth is the principle of material energy, including the sky and the physical universe. And the law of human signifies the principle to cause lives to rise and fall.

un-right thing must be exposed out as if brightness necessarily exists for the notion of darkness. Thus, humankind has developed by experiencing and looking at both sides for a while. As a result, it has reached the zenith, where any concept can be defined and shared with various examples.

For this reason, everybody has always suffered even if there is a brief moment of pleasure on earth. The law of Nature lets us know to live in harmony with others to eradicate the original sins, but we have not known it yet. When all humanity helps each other in the right way, Heaven, the energy of Nature existing itself, will allow us to live well together.

As long as all humans' sin is comprehended and removed, people and Gods will go back to the Grand Universe called as 'true self,' 'Atman,' 'Unity Consciousness,' or the home in which 70% of our energy stays. As a result, the physical universe will finish its job and disappear.

What we call original sin is, after all, a thing that we have made to claim and prove the concept of 'I' before the universe exists. Understanding it is the first way to eradicate original sin. Then, we should try to find and fix our problems to make others sacrificed. Thus, we need to awaken here to understand 'who I am' and 'why I was born'. And the last is to treat others right by getting rid of my karma. Finally, we will remove original sin with the correct efforts, and so the world will be filled with joy, wisdom, and happiness until the end of the world. It is possible only if we pursue altruistic life.

Chapter 4

New Humankind

The past of humankind has shown what matters occurred when people insist 'I,' ego, or self. Claiming 'I' refers to a life my desire leads. It corresponds to the phrase "I want." Psychologically, knowing my desire, means understanding myself better. So, those who know precisely their desire are more satisfied with their life than those who do not. Furthermore, they can accomplish the goal faster and more efficiently.

So, people would love to express, emphasize, assert, and show off 'me or myself.' Under the name of individuality and human rights, we respect each of the personalities and rights. For this reason, the culture and technology of the 21st century can have continuously developed. The result of this development indicates a variety of options in our life. When you order a Caffe latte in a coffee shop, diverse types of milk are available such as regular dairy, fat-free, low-fat, Lactose-free, soy milk, and almond breezes. It considers an individual's eating habits or allergies. This kind of service makes us feel respected and treated well.

Besides, people can create a new style by mixing the culture with familiar and unfamiliar ones. In this way, each individual can constitute a strong cultural identity of their own in the world. If such an individual's unique cultural qualities communicate with people, they become a worldwide star with the vast fandom of any nationality. Likewise, every culture worldwide is fused to complete the individual lifestyle, and finally, its boundaries disappear. Thus, the world becomes one, which is the culmination of life, insisting on 'I' from a cultural perspective.

When it comes to technology, it has been developed to make human life more convenient and efficient. For example, transportation has helped to move us to distant places, and other household appliances to save time and energy spent in maintaining daily lives. Furthermore, AI robots and the Internet will be free from physical labor and to have spiritual exchange with people around the world in their residence. It gives us time to focus more on self-development. However, it could be a double-sided blade that can let us be lazy or addicted to online games.

Anyhow, the goal of technology is to build a data ecosystem to provide a basis for humans to develop intellectually and mentally. As a result, it signifies that the environment for human growth is almost complete. Paradoxically, some people are afraid of AI's learning ability because a well-informed being is superior, as we know. So, some predict that the few who dominate AI will have real power, and the rest will become slaves to AI.

However, technology has made any service available to all humans. In other words, it will prevent the monopoly of knowledge. In this respect, anyone can access online to gain the information they need. It means whoever can be educated equally, and thus, citizenship worldwide can be growing altogether. It just divides into those who have encountered this circumstance first for self-development and those who have not yet. All the global surrounding setting up by science and technology does is to create the optimal conditions for human beings.

But there is a problem here. In the 2020 pandemic, Europe had to put up with many sacrifices to ensure human rights. The coronavirus broke the prejudice that an epidemic affects people in low countries. These phenomena would be good examples showing that we are missing something valuable. If people have developed themselves in a better environment, what should they do next?

Humanity has made tremendous progress through their individuality and talents but seems unable to find a way to the next. Do you still want to be rich, have power, or be famous? Suppose you have all of them, do you think you are seriously going to be happy with that, ignoring others dying from hunger and ignorance? Have you seen the news of the rich, celebrities, and politicians suffering from drug addiction, suicide, family feud, party addiction, and depression? People have been consistently proving by themselves that fulfilling the desire only for 'myself' is far from good consequences.

The purpose of the wealth, renown, and knowledge people have accomplished is definitely to help 'you'.

Therefore, only come out wisdom from humans, not AI. The reason we have developed 'I' as much as possible is to see 'You' as it is. Those who fully understand who 'I' am and what 'I' am can humbly put self or ego down. Then, wisdom comes out only when 'I' treat 'You' without 'my' discernment, thoughts, and emotions.

You are a prerequisite for the existence of I.

You are another I to be forced to be separat-

ed as an inevitable consequence.

You and I are one, not two.

For this reason, a new perspective from 'I' to 'You' will formulate a new order for the future. New humanity refers to those who benefit others. There are no English words that contain this meaning. So, I would like to borrow Korean, which has been using over the years. That is *Hongik Ingan* or 홍익인간(弘益人間), who will lead the world with wisdom by widely benefiting others.

So, in the future society, human beings will practice what machines cannot, but only correctly can humans do. For instance, AI doctors will treat the human physical body with up-to-date medical devices better than human doctors. Therefore, they will investigate the correlation between human emotions and thoughts and illness. Their research will uncover the root cause of what people talk about and act to cause disease. It could be genuine work for future doctors can do.

Likewise, judicial officers will inform us why people are embroiled in the lawsuit, and the AI judge will reach a valid verdict. Also, scientists will find the laws of immaterial like principles of the energy of words and knowledge, etc. Humanities will solve the question of family, husband and wife, workers, leaders, and every relationship. And they will explore ways to live in harmony by treating each other rightly. A new form of art with a narrative will emerge, reorganizing the art of the past.

All information will be disclosed, freeing people from physical threats. So, environmental safety will be guaranteed to create a mentally affluent society. For this reason, in some movies depicting the future, people externally look monotonous and uniform, but it is describing a highly mature and intelligent community.

To move forward on future society, we must change into altruistic life. Humanity will be able to complete a big step to peace when all abandon self and ego and then live for 'you'. Imagine how much the world will be joyful as a better place when everyone shares wisdom for each other on the street. It will be the future of humanity we will soon meet. And the future society will be clean and sober, no more senseless and emotional one.

Chapter 5.

Metacognition

I f a life of humankind in the future is like as I described above, which attributes do we have to become the new humankind? Human life easily clings to the desires of the body and, on the other side, depends on will or volition. The interest in the body seeks for its healthy, pleasant, and beautiful. So, each person can satisfy the desire for the body through different choices. It causes the body to change in every moment.

Besides, the will above the body's desire is related to the level of consciousness. In this way, some religious practitioners are willing to practice self-discipline beyond their desires, such as celibacy or fast. The consciousness through spirit can discern information and establish a new theory from a different point of view. It is an intrinsic property unique to humans. Due to this ability, humanity has been able to build up lots of knowledge so far.

Therefore, humans have both an animal element with desire and a decent human element with intellectual development. But some people try to fulfill their desires without ceasing. For instance, Manuel Uribe weighed

1,235 pounds (560Kg) according to Guinness World Record and passed away at 48. Cuba dictator Fidel Castro had 35,000 sexual partners, according to "The Sun". It is a measure of how inferior and greedy human desire can be performed since it does not happen in Nature. That is, the range of human desire is quite broad.

The human desire can be divided into three types: lower desires than animals, the same as animals, and transcendental desire. The lower desires than animals are subject to viruses, disease, and social detention. Animal lust instead helps the human body to function correctly. It proves that animals living without human intervention stay healthier than domestic ones. And the last transcendental desire is feasible in the right state of the consciousness, but otherwise, it would ruin the body system with extreme fasting and yoga.

In the meantime, humanity has been dominated with desire, but as new humankind will have metacognition, a new field of awareness will open. I would like to re-organize the existing meta-cognition and meta-emotion from the cognitive point of view. In addition to this concept, I want to include a meta-body. Hence, a more advanced future humanity with metacognition will emerge, which acts like a god that governs and controls a human body, emotion, and thoughts. Simply put, new humanity will be the most similar as a god who leads a human body adapted for a purpose.

Thought

When it comes to consciousness, departments such as psychology, psychoanalysis, and brain science have been studying for a long time. However, new humankind needs a higher level of consciousness to perform highly mature cognitive activities. It is called metacognition. It refers to "thinking about thinking" and was introduced as a concept by John Flavell, an American developmental psychologist. He stated that it is the knowledge you had of your cognitive process from an educational standpoint in 1979. In Buddhism, there exists a similar concept as 'Sati' or mindfulness, which means to pay attention to the present state of body, emotion, and thoughts from the third person point of view.

Metacognition enables us to cognize acts of consciousness or cognitive process objectively. It allows us to practice self-regulation and self-reflection simultaneously. It also encourages us to see ourselves as it is, and thus, we can work and learn more efficiently.

Psychology studies have shown that capability is only observed in the smartest group of students. But I believe, in the future, it will be an essential prerequisite for new humanity because it does not lead to judging you from a personal perspective but rather, contributes not separated by you and me.

Not discerning you from my perspective represents that I can treat you as you are. In other words, the metacognition will give you wisdom for some difficulties you are facing. Therefore, it is likely to improve our lifestyle on this planet to a higher level, even if it is not that easy to have it. For example, if you think while looking at the other person's shortcomings, the thoughts are usually not sorted. However, if you have metacognition, it will discern whether the view is a complaint or jealousy and then be aware of why such negative thought arises. This cognitive ability serves to reduce inconducive thinking and improve discernment.

First of all, 'I' need to see my thoughts staying away from my perspective. And then, 'I' have to be able to see both the cause and effect the thought will make. So, the cause of my thoughts must uphold a justification, and the results should be beneficial to both. As a result, the idea will be good for you and me for sure. These cognitive abilities arise very quickly and enable high levels of interaction.

Emotion

Meta-emotion is a term used by Gottman, Katz & Hooven to describe parents' reactions to their children's emotional displays. They defined meta-emotion philosophically as "parental attitudes toward emotion" in 2010. It refers to the "executive functions of emotion," which means it encompasses both feelings and thoughts about emotion.

However, it seems that meta-cognition and meta-emotion are not distinguished. Metacognition covers the whole range of thoughts, and meta-emotion involves thoughts and feelings. So, metacognition appears to be able to manage both scopes of thought. Hence, I would like to redefine meta-emotion here as the emotion of the feeling that metacognition perceives. It refers to the emotional state that recognizes the present sense.

Meta-emotion helps us to perceive the present feeling happening to oneself as it is. Then, the consciousness controls not to be agitated by the arisen feeling. For instance, when abused by someone, suppose 'I' feel anger right now, metacognition recognizes the rage. Then, a sense of compassion arises for me, grabbing a wave of wrath. As a higher level of emotion, meta-emotion can control the current emotional state. When you enter this state, feelings cannot sway your reality. Metacognition is aware that the disappearance of rough sensations and how the thoughts change in those feelings. Therefore, it could reduce accidents and negative energy caused by negative emotions and makes it easier to stay emotionally calm.

Producing negative emotions degrades society. For instance, if you have heard that a friend blame someone in anger, the negative energy the friend made is conveyed through you, and then, it would be unknowingly ejected in some situations. In this way, the negative energy is circulated and causes crimes and conflicts in family or society. By observing the feelings that have occurred to me one step away, we discern its causes and effects and then decide whether to let it disappear or be expressed for benefiting others. It is how meta-emotion works.

Body

As mentioned earlier, the body is like a container, clothes, or transportation that carries the soul in the present life. At the end of this life, 'I' have to throw it away, so this body is not mine, but rather it is like a house for a while. However, people cannot abandon their attachment to the body even after death because they consider it 'I'.

Everyone is beautiful and attractive when they are young. There is a Korean saying that if you are over 40, you have to be responsible for your face. It means that your true self is slowly revealed from over 40. So, if your spirit is not pure and bright, it is hard to expect a good impression, no matter how good cosmetics you have applied to your skin. After a certain period, the body is directly affected by the soul, so that not only the healthy body but also the growth of the soul leads a healthy life literally.

To keep the body healthy, we just use it as if primates use their bodies. Every living thing except human beings in nature knows appropriately the way to use it. While some people indulge in desires by violating the order of nature, another wants to go to a forest or beach when they feel disgusted by human greed. It is because our body wants to follow the law of nature, but humans mostly ignore the signals. If overeating, you feel terrible or even get sick. Despite that, you keep in eating and then look for digestant or regret it.

Once metacognition perceives the body, the moderation of the body will be embodied. I would like to call it meta-body not to get dragged by desire anymore. Proper eating, exercise, and sleep lead a healthy life, and as an adult, adequate sex, pregnancy, and childbirth will help body circulation with hormones. Energy circulation workout and meditation help the soul and body to circulate ideally together, and we will be able to escape from the pain of the body until death. It is the way you use the body as it is.

Metacognition needs a variety of knowledge, experiences, and truth. Knowledge and experience let us grasp circumstances, and then the law of truth puts it right. Therefore, new humanity will comprehend how to control thoughts, emotion, and body through metacognition with the correct order. They can take good care of themselves and then behave in ways that truly benefit others. That is the moment decent humans emerge, and the world will change with a full of wisdom, peace, and love.

Chapter 6

Widely Benefit

Humans

As new humankind accumulates knowledge and experience and acquires the truth, with metacognition, the true reflection of oneself will finally begin.

Who am I?
Why am I here?
What have I done?
What should I do?

Through these questions and answers, 'I' sincerely understand myself. The correct answer will show you how suffering the people are. The pain of others starts to be felt like mine, not others, and then 'I' am aware that we are initially one, not two. In this way, 'I' see you as it is, not you in my way. After that, 'I' sincerely ask myself what I should genuinely do for you.

What is enlightenment? Many people have historically practiced at temples or meditation centers in the world to gain illumination, staying away from family and friends. Also, some people have published books or teach others how to practice. However, there is still no convincing explanation of what it is and how to fulfill it.

In western philosophy, enlightenment was associated with gaining knowledge, and in Buddhism, it was related to ultimate wisdom, or the state to know all. Immanuel Kant said, "enlightenment is man's emergence from his self-incurred immaturity (1784)". In sum, enlightenment is a state of ultimate wisdom with lots of knowledge and experiences. And the state of awareness is to realize all of my problems out of ignorance and immaturity.

For instance, if you suffer from liars, what shall you do? The easiest way is to blame them. But if being the state of enlightenment, you know that the environment and situation for lying come from you. In other words, if you are stubborn and inflexible, even though you believe it is your virtue, other people are more likely to lie if it could be uncomfortable for you. So, the lie of others is a measure of my tolerance and generosity. In this case, eliminating my problem causing lying would be going on the path of enlightenment regardless of where you are.

It could be hard to believe, but 'I' am somewhat responsible for the bad things happening around even if 'I' am a victim. However, we conceptually and unsophisticatedly tend to place all the blame on injures. So, in a case where the criminal and police confront, the criminal goes for the offender first. But if the police killed the criminal for some reason, the police could turn into a villain. As long as society judges the case in this way, the crime will never diminish.

Like incidents resulting from our problems or faults, our impure thoughts are projected into some cases. In other words, it is like lying does not occur where there is no concept of lying in society. By analogy, we all open our own Pandora's box, forming all the ideas of the world. When we speak and act with the negative concept, the energy is gathered into an accident like a movie. For this reason, when looking at the terrible incident such as juvenile sex crime in the news, you may feel terrifying, goosebumps, heartaches, or sorrow since we are related to it. The negative energy that I have created at some point, could bring about the incident.

Therefore, now we all need enlightenment. First of all, we should find our wickedness we try to hide and not to admit and then see it as it is. If you indeed find it, you will recognize how to get rid of it by yourself. It will pave the way for new humankind with the ideal for widely benefiting all humans.

Help others

If you have followed my story so far, you may have guessed helping people could have a different point of view. To truly help others, it will be the priority of all to help 'myself' as a saying, 'Heaven helps those who help themselves'. If you have financially, mentally, or socially troubles, it never happens to help others. It is as if the blind want to help the deaf. Deaf people can see the obstacles, but the blind cannot. Despite that, the blind wants to help the deaf because they cannot hear the beautiful sound in the world. Those who do not lead a fulfilled life must not allow others, and instead, it could be slightly arrogant.

If being well aware of myself, 'I' am ready to help others. For example, when a woman tells me her difficulties, wisdom comes out, and thus, 'I' can lead her to the right way to live. If so, how can we help the poor? Sometimes, a charity advertises 'need your help', showing the sick and scrawny third-world children. After seeing the advertisement, many of us are pitiful and efficiently apply for regular donations to charities.

Is it indeed helping those poor children? With the fragmented side of poverty, suppose you simply allow them to satisfy their hunger, the children will get used to eating without effort. It also signifies that you are depriving them of the opportunity to think about as follows: what poverty is, what causes poverty, what to do to overcome it, and what to do not to be hungry again. In other words, by eliminating the chance to live on their own, we force them to fall into beings who need the help of others forever unless there is a proper education system. How can we say that 'I' helped someone?

Those who donate large amounts of money ponder their donation will produce good results. But if your lifestyle is far from benefiting society, the consequences you expect will not come true. The most fundamental way to help people in need is to make a better place where everyone lives well. However, if your life is disorderly, extravagant, or greedy, increasing social degeneration, no matter how much money you contribute, you have never helped others before.

Likewise, helping others could not be as easy as we think. It is because we must be able to see both the cause and effect of the difficulty and educate them to get through it, which, more specifically, means we lead them to change their mind before providing money or food. Once people all over the world come together under one ideal to widely benefit humans, we will be able to enter the last phase of the mental evolution in the name of new humankind, or Hongik Ingan.

Epilogue

What is the truth? It is the absolute, inevitable, and universal law of Nature. It is like humans are supposed to die. It happens to all without exception. The truth is to lead people to happiness by guiding them in the right way to live. Knowing the truth implies getting out of suffering.

However, the truth comes out after all the foolishness is revealed. It is like being able to solve problems only when all kinds of wickedness emerge in the world. As a family feud resolves only when an unfortunate incident occurs, we have seen so many devastating cases as we can say how humans can be.

For 'my' desires, 'my' interests, 'my' greed, and 'my' pleasure, while lots of sacrifices are made, there is no legitimate explanation to figure this situation out so far. Therefore, we need the truth, which can make everyone nod. With COVID-19, everyone is globally isolated to face a new obstacle. The globe needs new laws and orders for the future generation that will be commonly able to apply to everyone. It is the reason why I write this book. If you are desperately looking for the truth or the right way, this book will be your friend.

To introduce myself briefly, I am an ordinary housewife. At the university, I studied English literature, literary theory, psychology, and western philosophy. After marriage, I had a chance to read eastern philosophy. When I was little, I used to go to the church and read a bible. As an adult, I was baptized in Catholicism in the name of Sophia. In 2014, I had a chance to study Buddhism and participated in English translation Sutra, which is not published, thanks to my yoga teacher. In 2019, I coincidentally found Jungbub while searching on YouTube (jungbub2013).

These days, lots of people just want to show off to the public to get attention, and at first glance, I considered the master Chun-Gong (천공, 天公) to be one of them. But his theories were reliable and reasonable, and he was trying to overturn the common conceptions which humankind has built up for a long time. Interestingly, he does not seem to be afraid of breaking down popular ideas and religions, insisting that we live in a transitional period. I have never heard this kind of words or ideas up to now.

The master Chun-Gong was abandoned at the age of 4 and did not complete a formal educational curriculum. Therefore, his unsophisticated wording and appearance could be misconceived. I realized that he is telling us the truth beyond existing knowledge with solid theory and a feasible methodology. And it is worth listening to those who have lost hope in the future. He said each of us has all different kinds of gifts, and thus if we acquire the truth, our truth will emerge. I would be grateful if this book would reach out to your heart and alter your perspective. And I hope that your knowledge will meet the truth and bloom. As long as it puts together, a new law will be born to enlighten the world.

Now, intellectuals worldwide ought to awaken and gather to establish a new law not just for your country but for the whole world. If my little resonance is delivered to you, I hope that your soul, struggling in darkness and pain, will start over again to benefit humanity widely. It is the happy ending of the previous 'a tale for adults' I wish.

*The Holy Scriptures of Heaven

一 始 無 始 一 析 三 極 無 盡 本 天 一 一 地 一 二 人 一 三

<The Story of Heaven>

Sense, time, and space occur from nothing.

They are divided into three, which are stopgap measures but authentic.

Put Heaven on top with number 1.

Earth belongs to number 1 as number 2.

Human is number 3 represented as a critical factor in heaven and on earth.

一 積 十 鉅 無 匱 化 三 天 二 三 地 二 三 人 二 三 大 三
合 六 生 七 八 九 運

<The Story of Earth>

Ten laws, 1 to 10, regulate an invisible crate or this Universe.

Heaven and earth are in the energy of this planet, but Human use.

Therefore, Humans play a leading character by making use of two energy.

As the three are added up and go into a body represented as number 6, the same as the number of beasts, a life begins.

Beyond the Universe, 70% of the energy exists, consisting of the undefiled state where you should go back after getting rid of every karma you earned. It stands for number 7.

If you enlighten someone else, the energy of joy comes from the person. It is represented as number 8.

If the energy of number 8 puts together, it is getting bigger and becomes number 9.

In the last number 10, you will be remeasured by comparing the weight of your karma and the energy of the number 9 you have built.

三 四 酷 環 五 七 一 妙 衍 萬 往 萬 來 用 變 不 動 本 本
心 本 太 陽 二 明 人 中 天 地 一 一 終 無 終 一

<The Story of Human>

Human beings stay in the third dimension, and souls without a physical body in the fourth dimension.

They seem separate but coexist. Each realm is called numbers 3 and 4, respectively.

The third dimension is full of severity, and the fourth one is filled with resentment.

As soon as a soul and a body are united at birth, the energy of the mind generates. It enables human beings to live like homo sapiens with a conscience, standing for number 5.

Hence, adding the number 5 and 7 is the same as number 1.

Even if you come and go between the third and fourth dimensions over ten thousand times, no chance makes you get out of the crate unless your karma is annihilated.

Your nature is like the Sun.

Those who get life in Heaven and on earth are called humans existing between animals and gods.

Heaven and earth are not two but the one.

All discernment is only temporary expedient for understanding and destroying karma.

Neither beginning nor end exists.

CPSIA information can be obtained
at www.ICGtesting.com
Printed in the USA
LVHW071933281020
670024LV00021B/623/J